From the Air

Poems

ALAN LEW

Panui Poetry Series Editor:
Aubrey L. Glazer

PANUI
www.Panui.org
C/O BRANDSTETTER LAW, PC
201 Mission Street, Suite 1200
San Francisco, CA 94105

© 2022 Alan Lew
Cover Design: Elyssa N. Wortzman & Aubrey L. Glazer
Editing & typesetting: Aubrey L. Glazer
All rights reserved.
ISBN: 979-8-9851399-0-7

מוקדש לעילוי נשמת
הרב אברהם יוסף
בן ישעיהו ושייндל ז״ל
זָכַרְתִּי לָךְ חֶסֶד נְעוּרַיִךְ
(ירמיהו ב׳: ב׳)

י״ג חֶשְׁוָן תשי״ד - י״ז טֵבֵת תשס״ט

ת נ צ ב ה

Dedicated to the soul ascent of:
Rabbi Alan Jeffry Lew
"I recall favorably the compassion of your youthfulness"
(Jeremiah 2:2)

November 10, 1943 – January 12, 2009

May his soul be bound up in the infinite poem

THIS PUBLICATION WAS MADE POSSIBLE BY THE GENEROSITY OF THE FOLLOWING:

Dedicated in loving memory of Rabbi Alan Lew, *o.b.m.* by:

R. Dr. Aubrey L. Glazer & Dr. Elyssa N. Wortzman

Mark Gunther & Anne Krantz

Michael Bien

Glenn M. Chertow & Dara B. Nachmanoff

Mark D. Reiss, M.D. & Joan Reinhardt Reiss

Dedicated in memory of our classmate and friend
—Rabbi David Wolpe, Max Webb Senior Rabbi (Sinai Temple)

—Rabbi Elie Spitz, Rabbi Emeritus (Congregation B'nai Israel)

Howard Haberman
In memory of his brother, Eugene Carl Haberman, *o.b.m.*
זכר ליהודה בן אברהם הכהן ולאה
ת נ צ ב ה

Mark D. Meyer
In memory of his parents, Anna & Joseph Meyer, *o.b.m.*
ת נ צ ב ה

Nouzhan Sehati & Jeannine Rahimian
In honor of Benjamin's bar mitzvah

Gary Goldberg
In memory of his beloved wife of 43 years, Deborah ("Debbie") Minden, *o.b.m.*,
who transitioned from this realm of physical actuality on August 2, 2020
ת נ צ ב ה

Acclaim for *From The Air*

Rabbi Alan Lew was meant to pour poetry in the world: fusing his insights and his humor with a deep capacity to surprise and enlighten. These poems deliver that promise, and his lips whisper as we breathe new life into his words.

—**Rabbi Dr. Bradley Shavit Artson,** Roslyn and Abner Goldstine Dean's Chair Professor of Philosophy

A little jewel. How precious when an unpublished poetry piece by the late, great Rabbi Alan Lew comes to us enshrined in a mirroring of texts offered by writers, poets and spiritual teachers who may have been the closest to him: dear friend Fischer; his rabbinic successors Richmond and Glazer; and his life partner ad widow Jaffe— whose shining homages offer the reader keys to unpacking this very Zen, very Jewish treasure chest. A love letter to life between sky and earth, and a very timely wisdom piece, making it a must read for anyone on a spiritual journey!

—**Dr. Mira Niculescu,** Golda Meir Fellow (Hebrew University, Jerusalem)

It is difficult to love from the air. But Rabbi Alan Lew shows us how easy it is to love when air is all there is to life. He teaches us through his life, his practice, his poetry: to love we must become air. Empty of form, but full of compassion. Aware of mortality and fully human. Constantly letting go while holding fast to love, to justice, to the world. To love, we turn to his practice, his poetry, in *From the Air*.

—**Rabbi Jonathan Slater, DMinn,** former Senior Program Director (Institute for Jewish Spirituality); author of *Mindful Jewish Living: Compassionate Practice*; *A Partner in Holiness*

Like Basho in Baltimore, Leonard Cohen in the airport lounge, the late Alan Lew's mysticism and humor shimmer in these short, posthumous poems. Some observational, others intimate, they refract the emptiness/fullness of life into almost epigrammatic utterances of wonder and love.

—**Rabbi Dr. Jay Michaelson,** author of *Is:heretical Jewish poems &blessings*

The rewards of slowly reading, re-reading, and absorbing Alan Lew's *From the Air* are smiles of recognition and increased, authentic grounding.

—**Rabbi Elie Spitz,** Rabbi Emeritus (Congregation B'nai Israel); author of *Does the Soul Survive?*

This book might well be titled, *The Essential Alan.* His quirky, loving, funny, honest, humble and utterly distinctive soul speaks clearly through this posthumous collection of slight poems. Whether he writes about roosters, clouds, salmon or flight attendants, he is always writing about emptiness, perception, love, absurdity and death. One's heart is always buoyed when spending time with Alan; this book makes for a poignant last visit.

—**Rabbi Nancy Flam,** Co-founder National Center for Jewish Healing and Institute for Jewish Spirituality

This is poetry of awakening — penetrating and playful. In our changing and not-changing world, we are fortunate to have this unexpected poetic *schnaps* to help us see things clearly from the air and wake up even more.

—**Rabbi Schachar Orenstein**, Co-Director Aleph Canada, *Lev/Yoga Shul*

From the Air

TABLE OF CONTENTS

Acknowledgements	11
1. Preface: by Sherril Jaffe Lew	15
2. Introduction: Seeing Suchness of *Zot, Tathātā From the Air*: On the Lost Poetics of Lew by Aubrey L. Glazer	25
3. From the Air by Alan Lew	49
4. Poetic Postscript: On *From the Air* by Norman Fischer	119
5. *Hesped* (Eulogy): In memory of Rabbi Alan Lew, *o.b.m.* by Rabbi Dorothy Richman	127
About the Author	141

ACKNOWLEDGEMENTS

Panui is grateful for the ongoing support of the following:

Anonymous
Irwin & Rhona Kramer
Howard & Ryan Stotland
Gary Shapiro
Robert Kleinman
Pat Gordon

Rabbi Josh Jacobs-Velde   Dr. M. Michael Thaler

Stacey Levine   Marion Fonville   Glen Gilbert
Rabbi Jonathan Omer-Man   Dr. Ivan Ickovits
Dr. Bruce Glazer   Cheryl Morris

Lorne Jacobs &Rhona Bezonsky   Robert Levy
Rami Avraham Efal   Brendan Kwinter
Rabbi Shawn Zevit   Rabbi Yosef Goldman
Dr. Eitan Fishbane   Rabbi Eugene Fleischman Sotirescu
R. Dr. Joel Hecker   R. Dr. Ariel Evan Mayse
Rabbi Sherril Gilbert   Linda D. Davis
Ardele Lister   Danny Schultz   Arianna Yakirov

Preface

Preface

When I met and fell in love with Alan Lew, he was a poet. Then he became a rabbinical student and then a rabbi. What he learned from his studies and pastoral work flowed into his poetry. The demands on a congregational rabbi are never-ending and do not leave much space for writing poems. Alan used to write poetry in a notebook with a fountain pen during board meetings, pretending to be taking notes, but most of these poems were written in airports, when Alan was sitting at the gate, or in the air, as he travelled between places to teach or to attend conferences. Hence, the title of this collection.

Alan died in 2009, so it is from the air that he is speaking to us now. In that sense, the title is prophetic. You will see prophecy in many of these poems. True poems always have an element of prophecy, I have discovered.

These are short poems. Short and shorter. You will get that joke shortly. These poems are full of jokes, which disguise how grim they are, or rather, make the grimness worthwhile. These poems are modest and teach modesty. Take the first poem:

> A rooster crossed
> the river, crossed
> the river, yes!
> and let out
> a mighty crow,

> having no idea
> how he'd gotten
> there or why
> he had come.

There is a sense of triumph and power in the poem's first half that is knocked sideways by the last half. You will see this movement again in the poems that follow. You will also see this image of crossing a river again, this image of dying, again and again. These are poems of death's mystery, death's inexorability:

> Why do people
> Need to go
> From Charlotte, North
> Carolina to Baltimore
> Maryland, anyway?

This humble lyric must have been written when Alan was sitting at the gate at the airport in Baltimore, on his way home or on his way to somewhere else. Here, somewhere in between places, he is suddenly impressed by the everyday absurdity of the course of our lives. They seem purposeful while they move inevitably toward death. The question underneath the question of why we persist in going hither and thither when we will all end up in the same place is the unanswerable question —why do the people we love have to die?

Alan died unexpectedly and suddenly, when he was away from home, at a conference just outside Baltimore. He couldn't have known he was going to die there when he removed the cap from his fountainpen to pen these prophetic lines in which the placed he is fated to die away from home is linked to Charlotte, North Carolina, the place where a twelve-year-old girl in his congregation died away from home in an horrific accident. So the question of how God can allow a child to be taken is inside these words also. Suddenly the sign at the gate becomes a sign to all of us of the river we will all one day cross. And yet Alan tells us this in such a jovial manner. He makes it possible to bear it.

Another poem prophesying his own death begins "It was too early to leave." He wrote this flying home early from my Bennington graduation to attend to synagogue duties. The poem ends:

> I would never have enough time to
> love you. No matter how long
> I lived. I would have to
> leave long before I was finished.

This turned out to be true, alas. This is the tragedy hiding inside almost all love stories. One lover will almost certainly outlive the other. Other poems also arise out of moments of our life together. In one we are driving across the Golden Gate Bridge. It ends with an affirmation of the eternity of love:

> …You are riding shotgun, turquois
> Scarf, turquoise eyes, eternal smile.

Nothing has ever changed. Nothing is changing. But then we remember, this is a crossing, like crossing a river, and the poem ends, *Everything is also changing.* That is how I'd found his love to be—something eternal and immutable. And yet, Alan died.

Several poems use several real scenes from our married life as their material—from our wedding to the birth of our second child. "Lunch at the Café" is a spoof of the fact that poets, no matter how homely, and Alan was not homely, can always attract beautiful women. And then there is the poem within that poem, where the poet appropriates the encounter for his own use. And yet I took this as a love poem to me, as it depicts a game we once played over lunch.

The poem that begins "A lovely man was dying…:" comes out of Alan's pastoral work. He was assiduous about visiting the sick and being with people before operations. This was what God commands us to do, he believed, and yet, at the end of the poem, we also see he thinks this God who is so eager for us to do acts of lovingkindness might also smite us for no reason. These are the poles of what we know about God. These are poems about what we don't know.

Many of these poems are psychological, the way Buddhism is psychological:

>Here I am choosing
>Hurt, that sharp exquisite
>Pang on the heart.

These poems are deeply informed by the wisdom of Buddhism. The poem that begins "This is it..." presents a litany of painful circumstances, examples of the ordinary heartbreak each of us experiences and concludes:

> ...but why bother to make the
> best of it when this is
> It? Hold it in your hands
> While you can, precious treasure which
> Will never come your way again.

When I first met Alan, he used to recount to me all the pain he had endured at Buddhist *sesshins,* and what sitting with this pain had taught him. Later, as a congregational rabbi, he was witness to all his congregants' pain and he helped numberless people through their suffering. Pain is the subject of the poem that begins "Everything depends on." It concludes:

> ...This is
> the rule: nothing
> felt squarely hurts.

These words are supremely comforting, but then there are the poems that are not comforting but disquieting, mostly about the hurry of time towards death:

> Sitting in the restaurant at the
> end of the meal, I suddenly
> felt the time which had been
> continuously passing since we
> walked in off the sidewalk and

what a serious thing this was.

This realization of the inexorable passage of time culminates in the horror of a poem in which the poet is examining two photographs of himself taken ten years apart. It ends like this:

> …in between
> the two pictures, invisible in the eddying
> ether: a snapshot of Death, caught
> unawares on his way to a feast.

This theme recurs in this short poem:

> Some days you
> wake up and
> you just can't
> bear to see
> the way your
> wristwatch lies
> on your wrist
> one more time.

The poem that begins "The river flows from the mountain" brings back the river crossing motif once again. It concludes by saying that he:

> awoke one morning with a foretaste
> of this other bank; Exultation, as
> the world slipped away behind me,
> a terrifying cartoon spilling harmlessly back
> into the bottle of ink it
> had inhabited before it was imagined.

Once again, I see his premonition of his early death, but in respect to the Eternal, is life a terrifying cartoon? It is disconcerting to think so.

The image of ink returns here with an ink blot. He was writing with a fountain pen in a pressurized cabin, after all.

> How strangely, how serenely the puffs
> Of white cloud hang between heaven
> and earth, casting their ink blot
> shadow onto an innocent world.

I am always moved when I read this last line. I feel Alan's love of the world and in turn I am filled with love for the world.

Toward the end of this collection there is a poem in which Alan imagines the dissolution of his body after his death:

> Now cover me over.
> Let the dirt be my blanket.
> Let the earth take
> As long as it wants to reclaim me.
> Let its long, low kiss consume me,

That "long, low kiss" slays me, his widow, the one who will one day lie down next to him in the grave. Alan was the great love of my life. He helped me to look at death dead on, to see it as union again with all things. He showed me it was real. He blessed me with a sense of the eternal.

The last poem in this collection takes place in a cemetery. He has done one funeral after another. The wind has been strangely high:

> Then, while we were praying,
> Our skull caps, our words,
> Our clothing, even our bodies,
> Were all swept upwards
> Torn away from our idea
> Of what we were,

This is what his death was, a total upending. It seems this wind is God. It seems this wind is air, the air through which he speaks to me now. The poem ends:

> Afterwards, I myself
> Hurried off to the airport
> And into the sky.

Sherril Jaffe Lew
November 2021
San Francisco, California

Introduction:

Seeing Suchness of *Zot, Tathātā From the Air*: On the Lost Poetics of Lew

Introduction:
Seeing Suchness of *Zot, Tathātā From the Air*:
On the Lost Poetics of Lew

Brace yourself from wherever you find yourself—into the air or from the air— of this moment. You are about to enter into a time-space machine that will transport you from the air to the very air you are already breathing with deeper awareness. Letters from the air around imbue each of these words before you with the aroma of infinite possibilities: the words of gifted writer and Lew's widow, Sherril Jaffe who has written a truly powerful preface about her life partner of blessed memory; the poetic words of post-script by dear friend and collaborator, Zuketsu Norman Fischer, who is writing in situ his poetic reflections; and words from his rabbinic colleague and collaborator, Rabbi Dorothy Richman, sharing another window into their spiritual work together through her eulogy. And if you pay attention, you will notice fragments of Hebrew letters scattered here and there forming almost words, which will be addressed in due time below.

What I intend to share in my words at the outset are more general framing of the contributions of Rabbi Alan Lew, o.b.m., to the project and practice of spiritual awakening through poetry as a contemplative act, specifically how his poetry teaches us to see anew *From the Air* and how the Suchness of *Zot, Tathātā* (terms I will define shortly) enable such insightful vision for living.

Everybody lovingly recalls a moment in Rabbi Lew's cult classic, *This Is Real and You Are Completely Unprepared* that somehow spoke to them or catalyzed a deeper self-reflection *en route* to transformation. I find myself forever returning to this story attributed to "a certain rebbe" in the following parable as re-told by Rabbi Lew—

> "There was a certain rebbe whose disciple was deeply troubled. The rebbe took him out of the village to a deep, dark forest. Before they entered, the rebbe said to the student:
>
> 'As you are entering the forest, ask God to give you the answer to your dilemma, then forget about this prayer, because you must pay very close attention to the path through the forest. Otherwise you'll get lost and never come out of the forest alive.' So the student entered asking God for the answer to his struggle. As his rabbi had instructed him, he then devoted all of his attention to the path itself and lost himself in it. Soon he began to take great pleasure in his walk. He took pleasure in the working of his body as it found its own pace on the path and in the fall of his foot on the cool forest floor. He was taken by the space itself—a verdant mossy path of deep, brilliant green. When he finally came out of the forest, he was smiling broadly.

The rebbe asked, 'Did God give you an answer?'

The student started to weep. 'I forgot all about the question!' he said. 'I put all my attention on the path, and after a while I took so much pleasure in what was in front of my face that I forgot about the question altogether.'

'In that case,' the rebbe said, 'I would say that God gave you your answer'."[1]

This is an example of what we can call a classic Lew poetics that feels deeply inspired by a hasidic parable with its Zen courage of transcending and including the very path itself. In retelling the story it is evolving and becoming a living part of this infinite conversation which Rabbi Lew envisioned for Jewish spirituality. To illustrate the creative genius of pointing to the "suchness" of the path within this parable, I share just one of a handful of retellings of this hasidic parable,[2] here as retold by Yehiel Michel Stern:

---

[1] Alan Lew, *This Is Real and You Are Completely Unprepared,* (New York: Back Bay Books, Little, Brown and Company, 2018).

[2] To compare with other versions of this hasidic parable, see: R. Hayyim Halberstam of Sanz, *Darchai Hayyim: Imrot R. Hayyim Halberstam of Sanz* (R. Rafael Levi Segal Simatbiom Publications: Krakow, 1923), quoted in S.Y. Agnon, *Days of Awe*, (Schocken Books: New York, 1946), p. 27; R. Hayyim Halberstam of Sanz, *L'Hitaneg, Parshat Be'Ha'alotekha* (Ot haZahav: Har Nof, Jerusalem, n.d.), p. 62; see also ibid, *Hinukh Sanz*, vol. 6 (Sivan: Mossedot Hinukh Sanz, 1964), p. 11a.

Once there was a person wandering about in a forest for several days, not knowing how to find the right way out. We all know that feeling of being truly lost. Suddenly he saw a person approaching him. His heart was filled with joy.

"Now I shall certainly find out which is the right way," he thought to himself.

When they neared one another, he asked the stranger:

"Brother, tell me which is the right way. I have been wandering about in this forest for several days."

The other person said to him:

"Brother, I do not know the way out either. For I too have been wandering about here for many, many days. But the only advantage I have over you is that I can tell you which path not to follow [that will lead you astray]. "Look after the wellbeing of your friend" (Genesis 37:14)—When you look upon your friend, look at what s/he is lacking…someone who is arrogant cannot see what is lacking within oneself, and takes pride in what is not actually there.

> This person is like a rainbow whose splendor resides in its colors, and as soon as the sun gathers all its rays together, then immediately the rainbow disappears. For an arrogant person gets puffed up about inner qualities that are not there...[3]

How does the retelling of such a hasidic parable through Rabbi Lew's Zen lens point us to deeper awareness for living? Does the retelling foreground the pathless path while setting into relief the challenge of refining those pathways of spiritual qualia or distracting thoughts?[4] In listening deeply to this parable I hear something unique in the contemplative poetics of Rabbi Lew—a conversation between the Buddhist technique of *Tathātā* that realizes the "thusness" or "suchness" as the true, concrete essence or nature of things before ideas or words intersecting with the Jewish mystical reading of *Zot* in the Zohar that correlates "thusness" to the sphere of consciousness known as *Shekhinah*. It is in the primordial modality of prayer that Jewish mysticism evolves a tradition of embodying divine awareness, from medieval Zohar to modern hasidism. Prayer—

---

[3] R. Yehiel Michel Stern, *Sefer ha Mechanikh*, vol. 6 (Ezrat Torah: Jerusalem, 2003), 127.

[4] Rabbi Lew's retelling of this parable sets into relief its original telling by the Ba'al Shem Tov that is primarily concerned with pathways of thoughts and how the forest of the mind can lead to distracting thoughts, see Ba'al Shem Tov, *The Pillar of Prayer: Teachings of Contemplative Guidance in Prayer, Sacred Study, and the Spiritual Life from the Ba'al Shem Tov and His Circle*, tr. Menachem Kallus, ed. Aubrey L. Glazer (Louisville, KY: Fons Vitae, 2011), no. 89, pp. 108-109.

oftentimes like poetry—is primarily concerned with translating the unspoken into words, rolling light from with the darkness. Prayer— oftentimes like poetry— channels the primordial embodied feelings present in tears, laughter and melodies. What the Jewish mystical tradition enables is an expansive bridge between the divine mind and human mind. Standing on that bridge, one is positioned at the edge of consciousness while squarely in the midst of embodied life and living prayer. In what follows I will attempt to read this contemplative practice through the lost poetics of Rabbi Lew's *From the Air*.

From the Air is framed by a spiraling series of ascents and descents along the chariot of life through this unique Jewish-Zen lens that was part of a larger renaissance of Jewish meditation and spirituality that swept through the Bay Area in the 1990s. Rabbi Lew came to realize that the poetry he scribbled — whether while waiting in airports or weathering interminable synagogue board meetings — brought the Torah of Awareness into deeper attunement with his journey. Living a contemplative life meant that there was precious little time for writing in general and poetry in particular, yet Rabbi Lew managed to be a "holy thief" and steal the time necessary to think through and then write with the treasures he absconded with from the vast expanses of storehouse consciousness. While we may hear the voice of Rabbi Lew, of blessed memory, as if it were speaking to us from the great beyond, *From the Air,* there is something very direct in how this poetry discerns the discontent, suffering and death that we all confront and experience. The lost rooster that opens *From the Air* immediately jumps from a place of unknowing to the knowledge of a final vision preceding death:

> If this is
> the last thing
> I ever see,

But what Rabbi Lew beholds he yearns to see with utmost clarity, so that the veil always separating every person from the truth can be rent by a crystalline poetic vision. Clouds usually "cloud our vision" and yet paradoxically here Rabbi Lew sees how:

> these diaphanous clouds
> floating past a
> snow-dappled earth,
> let me see
> it well enough
> to catch the
> earth dissolving into
> pattern and life.

"To catch" the suchness of this fleeting "pattern and life" before us is the challenge of living amidst the dissolution of all things that come and go, birthing into the world, dying and taking leave of it only to be reborn *From the Air*. Am I really that different in the grand scheme of things from "a rooster" that "crossed the river"? If life is more than a joke about why the chicken crossed the road, and even why the rooster crossed the river, then will we ever really have some idea as to how we have gotten there or why we have come here altogether?

The rooster may not have the depth of consciousness that we have as humans, but we all know the feeling of exasperation and catharsis that comes from letting out "a mighty crow"—perhaps from that big-mind perspective of prayer? Whatever I may do to move through life from a lower state of unknowing to a higher state of knowing only then positions me to move to an even higher state of unknowing—so how different am I really from that river-crossing rooster after all?

And with suchness of this knowledge that what is here for the moment may be the last thing I see—whether I am going "From Charlotte, North/Carolina to Baltimore,/Maryland" — am I better equipped to navigate the challenges of life and somehow cope with all its suffering?

As Sherril points out, this poetic contemplation of all the oscillation of life actually become prophetic as Rabbi Lew passes in Baltimore, Maryland. Could the two of us, as rabbis have known that our very walk into the forest of the Pearlstone Retreat Center would be one of his last? If felt like he was always struggling to see clearly enough through the diaphanous clouds to be present to the suchness of our encounter—and so what stays with me to this moment is his quality of presence. It is an intensity of will to be present to uncontrollable suchness of each moment like it is your last. It demands a certain humility that begins in the submission to meditation and culminates in the ecstatic passion of poetry.

So when we read *From the Air*, keep this in mind, the intense curiosity of the quotidian that permeated his waking life, and by extension, each of our lives if we are willing to commit to the "suchness" of this seeing and listening, what Rilke imagined as "the hushed moments/when the nameless draws near."[5]. Rabbi Lew felt his calling as a poet and pastor through an intense seeing and listening to this "suchness". I wonder about the closing of *From the Air* and whether in either role— as a poet and pastor— Rabbi Lew felt God speaking to him through this this "suchness" of the diaphanous clouds? Something mysterious abides in the mundane, so that a quotidian flight on an airplane becomes a spiritual ascent that elevates all of material existence with it back to its source of the everyday even *From the Air*.

If the experience of the ineffable remains unknowable to most of us, then who better to turn to then, than that "…arresting combination of monk, mystic and mechanic,"[6] also known as Austrian émigré to Cambridge, Ludwig Wittgenstein (1889-1951). Recall Wittgenstein's koan of a concluding note to the masterful *Tractatus Philosophicus*: "Of that which one cannot know, it is best to remain silent."[7]

---

[5] Rainer M. Rilke, translated by Anita Barrows, and Joanna Macy. *Rilke's Book of Hours: Love Poems to God*, (Penguin: New York. 2005).

6 D. Edmonds & J. Eidinow, *Wittgenstein's Poker: The Story of a Ten-Minute Argument Between Two Great Philosophers*, HarperCollins, New York 2001, p. 22.

7 "*Wovon man nicht sprechen kann, darüber muss man schweigen,*" see L.Wittgenstein, *Tractatus-Logicus Philosophicus*, ed. G.E.M. Anscombe & G. H. von Wright, Basil Blackwell, Oxford 1967, no. 7, pp. 188-189.

Moreover, this brings me back to a certain aphorism—very akin to a Zen koan—that Wittgenstein also once wrote: " 'You can't hear God speak to someone else. You can hear him only if you are being addressed.' That is a grammatical remark."[8] Yet against all philosophic odds, *From the Air* enables the reader to "hear God speak to someone else"— through the poet, Rabbi Lew to each and every one of us in this reading moment.

Between knowing and unknowing, between the language of address and silence, it seems to me that the poetics of Rabbi Lew call every reader differently. This grammar of hearing or seeing God in our lives is a feeling of forever yearning and constantly burning inside the mystical experience of being human —why? "[M]ystical experiences may continue to flourish among human beings," as scholar of Jewish mysticism, Gershom Scholem (1897-1982) once remarked, "…so long as the human race exists because mysticism is a basic human experience, connected to the very nature of man [sic]." So if mysticism is woven into the very fabric of being human, when why do we remain so totally unprepared to receive its flow?

As one of the defining features of humanity, already in 1963 Scholem is re-reading this "Cosmic Consciousness" that continues to differentiate humans from other forms of life in the works of Richard M. Bucke (1837-1902) from the dawn of the twentieth century.

---

8 " '*Gott kannst du nicht mit einem Andern reden hören, sondern nur, wenn du der Angeredete bist.'—Das ist eine grammatische Bemerkung,*" see L. Wittgenstein, Zettel, ed. G.E.M. Anscombe & G. H. von Wright, Basil. Blackwell, Oxford 1967, no. 717, p. 124.

The shift from what Bucke categorizes as "Simple Consciousness" to "Self Consciousness" and then to "Cosmic Consciousness" is an important realization in the role that mystical experiences play within the evolutionary trajectory of human consciousness.[9] To have a consciousness of the cosmos implies an understanding "of the life and order of the universe."[10] Perhaps it is this consciousness of the cosmos that pulses throughout *From the Air*, a consciousness that is exemplified by a "...state of moral exaltation, an indescribable feeling of elevation, elation and joyousness, and a quickening of the moral sense... [w]ith these come, what may be called a sense of immortality, a consciousness of eternal life, not a conviction that he shall have this, but the consciousness that he [sic] has it already."[11] Already having such a "direct unmistakable intercourse"[12] between God and human beings is what marks the conscious component of this experience as cosmic. Perhaps it is this consciousness of the cosmos that pulses throughout *From the Air*. While Buddhists call this "storehouse consciousness" without any divine source, such a "direct unmistakable intercourse" between God and human[13] beings is what marks the conscious component of this experience at once at particularly Jewish and universally cosmic.[14]

---

9 R. M. Bucke, *Cosmic Consciousness: A Classic investigation of the development of man's mystic relation to the Infinite*, E. P. Dutton, New York 1969, p. 1.

10 R. M. Bucke, *Cosmic Consciousness*, p. 3.

11 ibid, p. 3.

12 ibid, p. 3.

13 ibid, p. 3.

The possibility of encountering and cultivating such mystical consciousness through any experience whatsoever is not something Bucke seems ready to question, despite the dearth of skepticism voiced by most philosophers. But our concern here is whether *From the Air* opens that door to the suchness of cosmic consciousness in the here and now?

Look at your life, see your death, confront your mortality and see if the suchness of this confrontation brings forth any deeper awareness or spark of curiosity about it all. Pay attention to how this poetry cycle, *From the Air*, closes with two the suchness moments embedded in the real life rabbi-poets live daily in the funerals. Being surrounded by "a high, cold wind" awakens the poet in every human being:

> I wondered why the wind was so high,
> What the meaning of it was.
> Then, while we were praying,
> Our skull caps, our words,
> Our clothing, even our bodies,
> Were all swept upwards
> Torn away from our idea
> Of what they were,
> Our hats deprived of even
> The comfortable assumption

---

[14] See the poem by Elliot R. Wolfson, "*ālaya-vijñāna*" in *Unveiling the Veil of Unveiling: Philosophical Aphorisms & Poems on Time, Language, Being, & Truth*, (Panui: San Francisco, 2021); see my comments on this poem regarding "storehouse consciousness" therein, Aubrey L. Glazer, "*Introduction:* "On the possibility of Truth in Wolfson's Melancholic Melancholy Science," ibid, pp. 14-18.

> That they should rest on our heads.
>
> Afterwards, I myself
> Hurried off to the airport
> And into the sky.

Whether one is a poet, a philosopher or a theologian—all of us feel at times as though we are being swept upwards by this "high, cold wind"—but have you ever stopped long enough to wonder "What the meaning of it was"? While it may be something less dramatic than God speaking to Job from whirlwind in that culminating moment of his search for the meaning of his suffering,[15] still we suffer. And as we suffer we yearn for further clarity than the ancient Job or modern Larry Gopnik[16] were willing to contemplate within the whirlwind of existence. To be truly human demands that we take the time to contemplate the whirlwinds *From the Air* that impact on our lives.

Being human can begin again when we incline the ear of the soul, akin to the poet, who still wonders about the wind and wants to see the pattern and life directly through the diaphanous veil of the clouds. Becoming human again requires each of us to remain unsatisfied with obscuring nature of the whirlwind which also sweeps upwards everything in its path into the sky—seek clarity. And on it rode the prophet, Elijah, as envisioned by the Zohar here:

---

[15] See Job 38:1 and 40:6.

[16] Larry Gopnik was modern Job recast by the Coen brothers as a midwestern American Jewish physics teacher who also confronts the whirlwind at the end of their film A Serious Man (2009).

> "**And Elijah was swept up into the sky in a whirlwind**" (II Kings 2:11). And on it [Job was answered] And YHVH answered Job from the whirlwind (Job 38:1). And because of this the rabbis taught in the Mishnah: "Who is heroic? The one who channels their inner drive." (m*Avot* 4:1). And there are those who are able to adorn their donkey, without unsettling its rider. It is in that sense that scripture states of Abraham: "**and he saddled his donkey**" (Genesis 22:3).
>
> And regarding the Messiah scripture states: "**A poor person, riding on a donkey**" (Zechariah 9:9)."[17]

Even Rabbi Lew, who often appeared skeptical of mysticism, as strange as it seems, would probably have found a kindred spirit in this mystical reflection of the Zohar—why? Both of their poetics are unafraid of being swept up into the sky and returning. The scene becomes even more surreal with the Zoharic image of each person in life finding how to navigate the journey as their soul rides their given animal presence:

> "And there is a dog, and a snake and a braying donkey which are ridden by a person. And immediately when a person recognizes which one that s/he rides, s/he is liable."[18]

---

[17] Zohar 3:238a:15.
[18] Zohar 3:238a:15.

So while Rabbi Lew may have been channeling his inner drive by writing poetry in airports, his poetic intuition was tapping into the Jewish collective unconscious so rife with spiritual archetypes, like Elijah, Job and Abraham, who embody this heroism of taking flight to the air from the air, riding upon any one of these animal presences. From the early mystics of the *Shiur Komah* circle to the late hasidic master of the Warsaw Ghetto, R. Kalonymous Kalmish Shapira ben Elimelekh of Piaseczno, z"l (1889-1943) — there remains an ever-present awareness of the deep imprint of that chariot from the air composed of Hebrew letters embodied from time to time in this world. This suggests another insight into Rabbi Lew's practice of "suchness" akin to quantum entanglement insofar as "[t]he letters are still there in the physical world, just in a coarser manifestation."[19] Perhaps those Hebrew letters fluttering through these very poems are fragments of that this chariot in this world.

To be heroic then is to be fully present to the "suchness" of different directions into which one is drawn by competing inner drives, symbolized as archetypes of the bestial impulse (dog), the shadow (snake) or the commanding self (donkey), and for Rabbi Lew as the awakening self (rooster).

---

[19] See R. Kalonymous Kalmish Shapira, *Derekh HaMelekeh, Parashat VaYeshev* (Va'ad Hasidai Piacezena Jerusalem: [1930] 1995) p. 53: "With the twenty two letters of the Aleph Bet, God created the world, and those letters are still there in creation but just coarser, and have been transformed into this-worldliness. And to the extent that the soul sees not just the letters and their forms in Torah but also sees the supernal light manifest in this worldly forms, then your body can sense the sacred in this world."

Amidst so many degrees of distraction along the pathway navigating through the forest of storehouse consciousness, there are lucid patterns in its luminal darkness, amidst the "diaphanous clouds" with Hebrew letters imbedded in this world so that the sensitive ones writing and reading poetry can "sense the sacred in this world."[20]

So while the various streams of those inner drives pulsing through us may lead to distraction, *From The Air* holds out the hope that one can "acquire patience without/Even meaning to." That hopefulness permeates the poetry at hand as it invites the reader to live more directly in the moment: "Any time,/Any place,/Even this one" which returns us to the question of suchness. If there are said to be seventy facets to each verse in Torah, then surely they are parallel of pregnant moments within existence inviting a deeper awareness. Pointing to the shimmering "suchness" in Hebrew is indicated by the simple mystery of the grammatical demonstrative known as *Zot* and *Ze*. The simplicity is complicated by the mystical association of feminine demonstrative *Zot* aligned with the sphere of divine consciousness known as *Shekhinah*.

To point to this suchness is to occupy the space of the post-secular tzaddik who still sits and contemplates the Time-That-Is-Coming in each and every moment by contemplating the verse:

---

[20] ibid, *Derekh HaMelekeh, Parashat VaYeshev*, p. 53.

"**This [*ze*] is my God and I will enshrine this One**" (Exodus 15:2). Matt elucidates the very "suchness" of the divine as follows: "*Shekhinah*, the divine female.... One of Her many names is זאת (*zot*), "this," perhaps because as the Divine Presence She is constantly right here...."[21] Being right here now, moment to moment, strikes a chord with many spiritual seekers even after the Age of Aquarius. What is unusual, however, is to suggest that awareness is also an authentically Jewish concern. Nothing is unusual in that yearning within the Jewish soul, according to Matt, who comments further regarding the Zoharic search for the "suchness" this encounter with the divine:

> "How, then, can we find God? A clue is provided by one of the many names of *Shekhinah*, the feminine aspect of God, the divine presence. She is called Ocean, Well, Garden, Apple Orchard. She is also called *Zot*, which means simply 'this.' God is right here, in this very moment, fresh and unexpected, taking you by surprise. God is *this*."[22]

---

[21] See *Zohar* III: 174a, Pritzker Edition Vol. 9, tr. Matt, p. 154, n. 7. On *Shekhinah* as *zot* (*this*), see *Zohar* 1:49b, 72a, 93b, 176b, 200b, 228a; 2:11b–12a, 37a–b, 39b, 50b–51a, 54b, 57a, 126b, 236b, 238b; 3:8b, 13b, 24a, 31a, 37b, 40b–41a, 48b, 52b–53b, 58b–59a, 60b, 62a, 76a, 79b, 108a, 115b, 145b–146a, 176a, 179b–180b, 201a, 250a, 297b, 299a.

[22] Daniel C. Matt, *God and the Big Bang: Discovering Harmony between Science and Spirituality* (2nd ed., Woodstock, Vermont: Jewish Lights, 2016), p. 157.

This sensitivity is not just medieval but also modern, namely, an openness to living in the "suchness" that emerges elsewhere in the Jewish mystical tradition, especially in hasidism. Recall how the project of early hasidism was to renew Eastern European Judaism from its slumber as it ossified into orthodoxy.[23] But where — if not *From the Air* — did this impulse emerge from? How bitter the irony that the very sites which rebirthed open-hearted pathways of the spirit through hasidic visionaries wandering in Oskop, Medzhybizh, Zhitomir, and Uman are now the very Ukrainian sites of such immense suffering and hopelessness as Putin's War rages on. How apt then that it is from Uman we encounter this very subtle sensitivity to the suffering song of life in the teachings of Reb Nachman of Bratzlav (1772-1810). This hasidic mystic sees and feels how the "suchness" of this song emerges as the voice of "my [personal] deliverance" in its perpetual correspondence with the divine awareness that sees us in our collective suffering.[24] Reb Nachman teaches us to contemplate how it is oftentimes the truth that in life, the more we suffer, the more we are seen and thus known by God.

The depth of poetry is expressed to the degree that the poet is aware of the suffering of humanity — that is the primordial phoneme of every song of life.

---

[23] For further extended reflections on this prayerful awareness, see Aubrey L. Glazer, "Chanted Prayers in Early Hasidism," *Marginalia* (February 25, 2022), see: https://themarginaliareview.com/chanted-prayers-in-early-hasidism/

[24] Reb Nachman of Bratzlav, *Likutei Moharan* 27:6:2.

It also demands that the poet embrace a certain economy of words, no matter how delicious each one. So in his discerning poetic lexicon Rabbi Lew begs the question: Why does this Buddhist technique of *Tathātā* that realizes the "suchness" as the true, concrete essence or nature of things prior to ideas or words remain so compelling for Jewish seekers? Throughout the poetry of his life, Rabbi Lew embodied the posture of the Jewish seeker employing this Buddhist technique of *Tathātā* in tandem to Zoharic *Ze/Zot* to traverse the pathless path. Such a poet is willing to sit with the darkness of this moment that may lead to light but remains as fearless as the Psalmist who walks **"through the valley of deepest darkness."**[25] It is this very courage to sit with the darkness of the suchness of life that makes this poetry so valiant, so direct and urgent. To see with deeper clarity the very suchness of life that we all encounter as human beings is the task that comes to us as we live, love and reincarnate our spirits *From the Air*!

Are we willing to respond to this **"stilling voice of silence"**[26] from within? As I read *From The Air*, that **"stilling voice of silence"**[27] strikes to the core of my being as I also presided over funerals in Colma, San Francisco,[28] where both Rabbi Lew and myself were deployed to cross-over like the rooster.

---

[25] Psalm 23:4, often translated as the **"valley of the shadow of death"** as per King James translation.

[26] I Kings 19:12.

[27] I Kings 19:12.

Whenever officiating at the cemetery in Colma, I had the spiritual practice of visiting and meditating at tombstone right there where he is buried. My soul-to-soul check-in with Rabbi Lew was a spiritual renewing that **"stilling voice of silence"**[29] before being swept up into the air at other funerals nearby. It was a reminder to re-align myself to live more fully attuned to that prophetic **"compassion of your youthfulness"**[30] as inscribed on his tombstone. In a way, *From The Air* is really just a poetic "cord of compassion"[31] that extends throughout Rabbi Lew's life lived as a poem into our own.

Who would dare, after all, to cross that river without being attached to this "cord of compassion"? It really takes a raging rooster or any other courageous boundary-crosser to act as an *'Ivri* who is ready to cross the river "having no idea" in mind. Crossing the river is a poetic act—whether it is the River Yabok or Sambatyon— the godwrestler who dares crossing the abyss always needs to have that "cord of compassion" to hold onto.

---

[28] Colma (Ohlone for "Springs") is a small town in San Mateo County, California, on the San Francisco Peninsula, where many Jewish cemeteries are located at which we both officiated at countless funerals.

[29] I Kings 19:12.

[30] Jeremiah 2:2.

[31] This "thread of divine compassion" is said to connect to those who are constantly engaged in Torah Study, see Maimonides, *Mishneh Torah*, Torah Study, 3:13.

Poetry is really exemplified by such a river-crossing river of this-worldly consciousness into what the Buddhists experience as "storehouse consciousness".[32] This boundary crossing is a process of emptying the self to then refill with a more deeply discerned desire to be a channel aligned with the will of the One. When the poet declares, "If this is/the last thing/I ever see" it co- emerges *From The Air* of all inter-being because Rabbi Lew's poetic vision of the quotidian dares to toggle back and forth from within the very place of this liminal crossing.

I trust we can now see how "the last thing/I ever see" through "these diaphanous clouds" is really only possible *From The Air*. And such seeing is in relation to the "snow-dappled earth" which itself is "dissolving into/pattern and life," so that figure and ground are constantly oscillating and co-emerging in suchness. The poem momentarily flutters into that tender place of prayerful poetics when the poet beckons the source of inspiration: "let me see/it well enough/to catch..." That is the prayer of every poet—to grasp for whatever time allows the ungraspable, to touch the untouchable, to write the ineffable. Is every poet a mystic? Is every poet a Jew?[33] Can a Zen rabbi escape being a poet?

---

[32] Regarding *ālaya-vijñāna* known as "storehouse consciousness" see above n.14.

[33] For a more thorough rumination on this question of the Jew as poet, see Harry Fox, Preface, "Poet*h*ics: How Every Poet is a Jew," in Aubrey L. Glazer, *Contemporary Hebrew Mystical Poetry: How It Redeems Jewish Thinking*. (Lewiston, NY: Edwin Mellen Press, 2009), pp. i-xxxiv.

Rabbi Lew's teachings and meditations were always suspicious of mystical ecstasy and its possible abandonment of the ethical grounded in this world as evinced so lucidly in his prayerful caveat:

> Praise God,
> not letting any
> of it stick,
> not the praise
> nor even God.

We are left with a most simplex of prayerful poems meant to be posted on every lintel, inscribed on every head and heart, keeping us real even if we feel unprepared by heeding the warning of this Zen rabbi — never lose sight of direct "suchness" embedded in this daily life experienced *From The Air*—not even if God distracts you from that focus on "the emptiness at your center."

Aubrey L. Glazer, *Panui*
10th of Adar II, 5782
(Montréal/San Francisco)

From the Air

A rooster crossed
the river, crossed
the river, yes!
and let out
a mighty crow,
having no idea
how he'd gotten
there or why
he had come.

*

If this is
the last thing
I ever see,
these diaphanous clouds
floating past a
snow-dappled earth,
let me see
it well enough
to catch the
earth dissolving into
pattern and life.

*

Why do people
Need to go
From Charlotte, North
Carolina to Baltimore,
Maryland, anyway?

*

7

Now I remember
the light which holds everything up
like a curtain hung across the void
or a map we pull down
but then come to believe in,
the small, colored countries
become real places to us
which we then inhabit,
each with its own light,
its source; its distinctiveness,
its own map pulled down
over its particular void.

*

A room full of Jews in
Newark, New Jersey, waiting to fly
to Israel in a time of
danger. Tired and depressed, young and
old, dark and light, short and
shorter, every outfit a theological discourse,
everyone pushing ahead at the gate,
every soul exposed; my people, the
ones who never learned to hide
their hearts. I'm ashamed to think
there ever was a time I
could have failed to love them.

*

Remember to secure
Your own mask
Before helping others.

*

כ״ז

New Jersey from the air:
Oh my God, it's worse than I thought!

*

Serving drinks, the flight attendant's face
is lost in service, impossible to
know anything about him except that
he serves, his face fixed on
the drink he is pouring, his
cheek muscles releasing when it is
finally all poured out, the barest
suggestion of a smile coming to
the corners of his mouth then.

*

Movie time on the eastbound flight;
two figures on the big screen
emoting, arms gesticulating, heads bobbing, necks
twisting, torsos turning, faces flushed with
imagined feeling, actors, once flesh and
blood in a studio somewhere, now
merely lights on a screen. We
make these lights a human drama.
The feeling, even the figures themselves
only an exertion, an imposition of
mind on this light. Next to
the screen, a stewardess bends over
a passenger, hardly larger than the
actors on the screen, her figure
only slightly less yellow, more dense,
her feelings equally invented and empty.

*

א

Leaving the house at dawn,
with the streets still dark and silent,
the houses dark except
for an occasional kitchen light,
a single car starting up down the street,
an egg-shell light seeping into the sky,
one can hear God counting the stars by name,
tenderly calling their names,
the way I would call your name
if you weren't here.

*

I am driving. The Band is
playing "Unfaithful Servant" and Rag Moma
Rag." The homeless woman on the
parkway divider is begging for money.
The traffic is flowing. The fog
on the Golden Gateway is lifting.
Two women, one of them blonde,
are walking across the Golden Gate
Bridge. You are riding shotgun, turquoise
scarf, turquoise eyes, eternal smile.
Nothing has ever changed. Nothing is changing.
Everything is also changing.

*

Lunch at the Café

Do you come here often? she said.
Only when there are beautiful women here, he said.
When is that? she said.
Whenever you are here, he said.
But I am not women. I am a woman, she said.
When you come here once, you are a woman, he said.
When you come here twice, you are women.
Are you a poet? she said.
Yes, he said, would you like to hear my latest poem?

> Do you come here often? she said.
> Only when there are beautiful women here,
>   he said.
> When is that? she said.
> Whenever you are here, he said.

*

Last night as
we lay spooning
your back against
my rib cage
I felt a
heart beating and
I didn't know
whose it was.

Last night as
we lay spooning
your back pressed
close against my
chest, I felt
your rib cage
heaving, light and
transparent, beneath your
translucent skin. I
felt a big heart
beating and I
didn't know
whose it was.

*

The moment I awoke, I thought we
were clouds draped fluidly
across the bed, the white covers,
a flow of billows and folds, like
a sea of cloud seen from
the window of a plane.

The next moment, we were a
man and woman, happily
sprawled under animal skins,
a great fire warming
the cave and a satiety
filling our bellies.

*

Sitting across from you, your red,
red lips, your pale skin, your
golden hair floating above your bright
red sweater, your face first softening,
then dissolving, then dividing into several
faces, each of them infinitely familiar,
I feel a terror at how
far back this goes and how
bottomless it is, as if in
this I am not precisely me
but something unknown and beyond that
from before I was born. This
is how it will be when
we're dead, you say, and I
don't know if you mean the
love, the terror, the dissolving,
the sitting, or the bright red sweater.

*

א

Even if your teeth all
fell out and all of
your hair, and several of
your limbs were amputated, and
your heart was removed, and
you lost all your toes
one by one, I would
still never leave you. It
would hardly be necessary.

ב

Even if all your teeth
fell out and each of
your hairs one by one,
and several of your internal
organs were removed and one
of your arms and one
of your legs, and you
lost all your toes, we
would still make love
twice a week.

ג

If you lost your penis
and one of your testicles,
it would be all over
between us, but I would
still keep your heart in
a jar by the side of the bed.

ה

On the way to the hospital
for the birth of our second daughter, we drove across
a railroad track.

The contractions were fierce.
I was trying very hard to drive smoothly,
afraid the bumps would hurt you.

I felt you stiffen as we crossed the tracks.
You didn't answer when I asked you how you were.
As soon as we got to the hospital, you gave birth.

Now, when I think of that night,
the first thought that always arises
is of that moment when we crossed the tracks,

My desperation to keep the ride smooth,
my fear of causing you pain, and your silence,
the sea which gave us life.

*

One night in
Alaska, the moon
rose bright yellow
over Windfall Island,
a shower of
fiery meteors fell
softly from the
sky, the Northern
Lights spread from
horizon to horizon
half way up
the sky, sending
tendrils of light
down to the
rim of the
earth. Wolves howled,
loons hooted, salmon
leapt out of
the water and
splashed down again,
whales breathed deep
in the sea,
and the stars
whispered their silent,
endless secrets while
the mountains sat
listening quietly in
long solemn rows
like jurors considering
testimony.
All of
this took place
in the same

tender fastness of
the heart where
I keep you.

        *

א

Even now, more than
twenty years later,
I run into people
who say they were
there and I'm surprised. I don't
remember what the rabbi said.
I don't remember the toasts,
or if there were any toasts.
I don't remember the gifts.

What I remember is the rain,
the angels crying tears of joy,
the rain falling in great silver sheets,
and the house full of
everyone we knew,
and the fire going
and the dog asleep
in front of the fire,
and our four closet friends
on tip toes to hold up the *chuppah*
as if straining to hold up
the four corners of the world,

And the rabbi,
intoning the ancient spells
for opening the gates to eternity,
and you, of course,
strong and upright,
clear and fair before the everlasting fire,
standing in a shell of light while the silver sheets of
rain stormed down all around us.

*

It was too early to leave.
Nothing, not even my having come
several days early, could ever change
that or make it any less
painful. We embraced. I threw my
suitcase in the trunk. You walked
away. I called to you, blew
you a kiss when you turned
around, drove off without knowing you'd
come all the way back to
the car. I saw you in
the rearview mirror, standing there
in full erotic dignity; green
dress of enchantment, golden curls, full
golden face ripe with love and
with disappointment. It was then that
I knew for a certainty; I
would never have enough time to
love you. No matter how long
I lived. I would have to
leave long before I was finished.

*

In the first picture, I am
forty-seven. Except for a touch
of silver at the tip of
my brow, my hair is still
black. I am fit and thin.
In the second picture, taken ten
years later, there is silver all
over my hair, and my body
has sagged some. The bones have
aged; the skin seems to rest
more loosely on them. In between
the two pictures, invisible in the eddying
ether; a snapshot of Death, caught
unawares on his way to a feast.

*

The urge for justice and justification,
to fix what we can't fix
to right what we can't right,
arises incessantly and rages on. No
sense in trying to stop it.
We need to climb inside and try to make it better. We
can't. Better just to watch it
rise up from our bodily symmetry,
out of our two ears, approximately
equal in size and in shape,
one on each side of the
head, and the same with our shoulder-
blades and our breasts. Better just
to watch the urge for justice
rise up out of our biology,
and then float away as the
breath floats away, like the body, a
thing of beauty which doesn't last.

*

A lovely man was dying. I
went to see him in the
hospital. Coming out, I was tempted
to walk the labyrinth in the
courtyard, but the sun was blazing
down on it as if focused
through a magnifying glass the way
we used to do to the
insect world when we were kids.

*

Bright day, high wind, few people
present when she was laid to
rest, this woman who had played
golf and tennis, graduated from high
school three years early, earned advanced
degrees in mathematics, installed computers for
a large insurance firm years before
their time. Everyone called her Aunt
Lil. She taught her two nephews
to drive long before they were
of legal age. One of them
was so small his feet wouldn't
reach the floorboard. "What I'm going to remember
most of all," he
told the nine adults and two
little girls in attendance, "are the
phone calls. She called me twice
every day to tell me she
loved me." He put his right
hand on his heart as if
he were pledging allegiance. Each of
the mourners shoveled some dirt into
the grave. There was barely enough
to disturb the shiny brown surface
of the coffin. The cemetery workers
asked them if they wanted to
watch them fill in the grave
but they said no. They went
off to their cars instead, pausing
only briefly in the bright sun,
in the cool, twisting wind to
converse, then driving off in three

separate cars, having made no arrangement
to comfort one another later on.

*

Watching the living
shovel earth on
the dead, it
is unclear if
this is a
gesture of caring
or bravado. Only
one woman, the
philipina caretaker, weeps
as she relinquishes
the shovel. Everyone
else struggles to
express their mastery
of the dead,
of death itself.
A few of
them stumble on
the narrow pathway
to the grave.
One presses his
palm against the
top of his
brow as if
trying to contain
something which will
not be contained.

*

Sitting in the restaurant at the end of the meal, I suddenly felt the time which had been continuously passing since we walked in off the sidewalk and what a serious thing this was.

*

All frozen up with fear, I
will go out to the streets
again to see if the great
river is still flowing, the cars,
the bodies moving at inconceivable angles
the great foggy dazzle spreading east
from the ocean; traffic, commerce, weather.

*

Sunday afternoon at Folsom Prison,
stacks and stacks of men
in cages, two to a cell,
lying on their bunk beds
wearing white underwear, their
cells so small only one
of them can stand at
a time, an exposed, metal
toilet in the middle of
the floor, and a color
TV lit and flickering at
the foot of each bed,
this one tuned to a
basketball game, this one to
golf; someone kneeling intently to
line up a putt on
a long green; someone else
striding briskly up the fairway.

*

ב

Humans are funny
the way they
take so much
pleasure in saying
things to each
other like
happy new year
and good morning.

*

Just the light coming out of
the lamp, an inverted fan above
the shadow line, hard and bright
on the white painted pipe behind
the lamp, gradually fading to ambient
light on either side, then a
gentler brightness near the window, the
muted light of a grey morning.

Just this light on a wide
white wall and nothing beyond it.

*

Chin in hand, elbow resting
on the windowsill, mind a
spiraled focus; before it, rain
on the window, lights flashing
on the rain-slicked runway.
Behind it in the waiting
room, a cloud of conversation,
people speaking of dreams, the
unanswered ringing of a telephone.

*

A big window close to the
highway the heater drowning out the
sound of the cars so that
they are only seen, quite large
and soundlessly gliding by, one thought
relentlessly pursuing another in two directions.

*

Everything depends on
where one puts
the mind or
on being awake
enough to remember
to put it
somewhere. Pain is
merely what the
things we don't
like feel like
when we aren't
feeling them. Fixing
them flush, letting
them fill the
full sphere of
awareness, we stop
disliking them; we
see them for
the lustrous centers
of sensation they
are. This is
the rule; nothing
felt squarely hurts.

*

This is it. You can almost
hold it in your hands, the
irredeemable, unsupportable pain others only speak
of as a theological proposition. The
diminishing child who you can't help,
the mother sinking slowly into inaccessibility,
the house you grew up in
suddenly sold out from under you
leaving you adrift in space. Making
the best of it you could
say this drift is the truth;
your mother never really gave you
anything anyway and your hopes for
your son were just foolish projections,
but why bother to make the
best of it when this is
it? Hold it in your hands
while you can, precious treasure which
will never come your way again.

*

ה

Deep inside
someone else's soul
one-hundred
stray wings are
beating. I can't
imagine this

*

Here I am choosing
hurt, that sharp exquisite
pang on the heart.

*

וייס

All these years,
Waiting to see who I was,
Waiting for the strength in that.

What a joke!
All the while
I was the waiting
And the strength was
In being everything
I was not.

*

Right field at
Pac Bell Park
On the bay,
a high brick
wall, people packed
on top of
it in orderly
rows, only the
abrupt horizon behind
them, a pale
blue nothing—where
they are actually
going! even though
they've turned their
backs on it
and are facing
the field, mesmerized
by the game
being played there.

*

Sitting upstairs,
hearing a soft, indistinct
voice down below,
it seems as
if the house
were trying to
speak, its walls
vibrating softly like
a throat. Then
the voice stopped,
the house fell
silent again, and
one could feel
the unspoken stuck
in its walls.

*

Tossing and turning late at night,
constricted, tormented by jealousy and rage,
I suddenly awoke to these feelings,
felt them, became them all at one, understood
this awakening to them as a
grace, a release from the pain
and the suffering of them, the
anger and jealousy no longer oppressive
but merely the fuel for this
sudden eruption of pure freedom.

*

As soon as he spawns, the salmon loses his life
force and begins to disintegrate,
but the end begins well
before that. Just before spawning,
the salmon become so desperate
for females that they fight
each other for them savagely. They
tear each other to shreds. Their
jaws become set in a
permanent arc of rage and
they begin to turn black.
The spawning itself is an
anticlimax. Then they dissolve into
the sea and the earth.
Their molecules can be found
in the nearby trees and
in the bodies of those
who eat them and, of
course, in their descendants who
continue to rage up the
rivers to the spawning fields.

*

After twenty minutes of Yoga, forty-five
minutes of meditation, forty minutes of
prayer, a half-hour of exercise and
a half-hour bath, I felt
pretty good for a few minutes.

*

Most of the time we are
half aware of the music, letting
it float in and out of
our awareness and our mood. When
we focus on it, following the
flow of the notes, we begin
to discern mysterious forms, shapes
we can't quite fathom, opening before us
in lines. But it's when we
are not aware of the music
at all that it touches us
most deeply, fathoming us without effort,
entering us without any resistance.

*

The river flows from the mountain
to the sea where it joins
all the rivers and the waters
which have rained down from the
sky and the waters which were
already there before creation, all of
it rising and falling in billows
and waves as it always has.
Sometimes the river flows in rapids and sometimes in
trickling streams so faint they barely sustain the flow
And we worry about this, forgetting
that the most significant movement is
not from the mountain to the
sea, but from one bank of
the river to the other, the
journey Siddhartha made at the end
of his days after life had
disabused him of every ambition except
to ferry his fellow creatures back
and forth across the river, seeing
in this finally an instance of
the greater crossing, or Jacob who
suddenly awoke, left his entire household
on one side of the Yabok
and then crossed to the other
to confront his own darkness at
last, emerging wounded but convinced he
had seen the face of God. I
awoke one morning with a foretaste
of this other bank ; Exultation, as
the world slipped away behind me,

a terrifying cartoon spilling harmlessly back
into the bottle of ink it
had inhabited before it was imagined.

*

I finally realized why we love
Willie Mays so much, why we
won't even consider the possibility that
anyone could have been his equal
on the baseball field. It is
because when he made that impossible
catch in the 1954 World Series,
when he ran after that ball
Dick Wertz hit high and long
into the deepest center-field there ever
was, when he ran, back turned
to home, his herky-jerky grace, his
exuberance tuned to a laser point,
his cap bouncing and finally falling
off his head altogether, his flannel
uniform flapping all around him as
if it were trying to keep
from being left behind—he looked
as if he were running right
out of his body exactly as
we had always longed to do.

*

Standing on a treadmill for my
stress test, I looked over at
the sonogram monitor and saw my
own heart beating. Its chambers looked
like animated clay figures, two gumbies,
dimly seen in a darkness, convulsing
violently, bending at the waist, a
hole opening wide in each of
their chests and then closing again
with every beat of my heart.
These gestures were desperate, the kind
one summons to meet the final
catastrophe, the expenditure of one's last
desperate jot. Was this going on
beneath my ribs all the time
or was I suddenly dying; was
my vital muscle about to explode?
Perfectly normal, the cardiologist said, ripping
the electrodes off my chest and
then hurrying out of the room.

*

The house is dark and still.
The bills are paid. Outside the
streets are finally drenched with rain
after a long, dry winter. Yesterday,
I noticed I hadn't watered the
plant for far too long. It
looked dead. I watered it anyway.
I cupped my hands down
a few inches over the drooping
leaves and felt the life in
between. Now it is raining. A
piano is playing, chords and crescendos
cascading down. The house is dark
and still. The bills are paid.

*

Prayer

Fill it up.
Please fill it up.
Oh please fill it up;
the emptiness at your center.

*

When the Red
Sea split, God
slipped into this
world through the cracks. Assumptions
arose the instant
He arrived: He
would be male;
He would be
a Man of
War; He would
dislike Egyptians. Such
things are inevitable
here where nothing
can exist without
being reduced or
mistaken for something
It is not.

*

Dark silver day,
fat woman, black
halter top, blonde
pony tail, walking
alone on the
asphalt shoulder of
Highway Seven where
it crosses the
TommaHannok Reservoir, emerald
green water, emerald
woods all around
her, black clouds,
silver sky above.

*

7

Looking at the
falls as a whole,
the water appears
to be rushing
down with frightening
force but focusing
on any particular
fragment, any moment,
this water seems
lost in a
feathery free-fall,
having finally let
go, having shaken
loose from gravity's
terrible hold, falling
lightly and slowly
forever, God's dream.

*

You will love
God with every
feeling, every impulse,
every breath, in
the rising up
and the falling
away, let every
breath praise God,
let the fear
of failure praise
God, let the
conviction that you
don't deserve respect
praise God, let
the mind wandering
when you begin
to feel the
full power of
being alive praise
God, let every
breath praise God,
every rise, every
fall, becoming each
impulse completely without
letting it become
who you are.
Become who you
are. You are
very far beyond
the rise and
fall. Praise God,

not letting any
of it stick,
not the praise
nor even God.

*

At the end of the day
in spite of the cartilage and
bone aching in the back and
the knee and the roll of
fat around the belly, one feels
one is made of light, one
feels the column of light in
the spine holding one aloft and
the terror of being so insubstantial.

*

Some days you
wake up and
you just can't
bear to see
the way your
wristwatch lies
on your wrist
one more time

        *

When the mourners were saying
the Kadish, a fullness came
over me; the sounds on
the air inhabiting me fully,
pushing out against my
shaking, jagged edges
and then breaking free

*

Airport morning, all things wait expectantly;
parked planes, oversized hangars planted on
the airfield like great cats at
rest. The sun, just rising over
the eastern hills, spreads a soft
golden cloak over everything. One plane
nose down, a flying insect wings
not yet fully unfurled, rolls slowly
down the runway barely awakened to
the imperatives of day. Paper cup
full of coffee. Taut green surface
of the bay gathering golden light.
Soul brimming with possibilities. The plane
borrows force from the sleeping hills
and finally breaks free of the
earth, lifting itself skyward to join
the blue firmament, the golden sun.

*

י"א

Squeezed between two
Big shouldered men,
Belly bulging over my belt,
Sweat on my brow
And my forearm,
Shirt soaked
From the effort of
Stuffing the suitcase
Into the
Overhead compartment;
The body doesn't love itself.
Soon it will itch.
But for now,
As the engines rev up
And we hurtle down the run-way,
It is all that I have.

*

Looking down on
us, surveying creation
from the infinite
perspective of the
Divine Throne, God
doesn't really care
that we watch
so much television
nor prefer that
we listen to
classical music instead.

                      *

Night shower, bright
lights falling from
the sky, little
airplanes coming home
to an airport
by the sea.

     *

How strangely, how serenely the puffs
of white cloud hang between heaven
and earth, casting their ink blot
shadow onto an innocent world.

*

ייזט

Don't burn this body.
Let it melt slowly down
The way my life went.

Perhaps I should have burned
But having lacked the courage
Let the earth take me
On its own terms,
In its own time.

Waiting to burn
But never burning
I acquire patience without
Even meaning to.

Now cover me over.
Let the dirt be my blanket.
Let the earth take
As long as it wants to reclaim me.
Let its long, low kiss consume me,

A fire itself
When seen from a great distance
Its duration reduced to a
Fiery moment by eternity.

*

Any time,
    Any place,
        Even this one.

                *

י"ג

I did one funeral
Then another an hour later,
The people were arriving
For the second
Before the first was over.

There was a high, cold wind.
No one wanted to tarry. A young boy
Kept stepping on the graves.

I wondered why the wind was so high,
What the meaning of it was.
Then, while we were praying,
Our skull caps, our words,
Our clothing, even our bodies,
Were all swept upwards
Torn away from our idea
Of what they were,
Our hats deprived of even
The comfortable assumption
That they should rest on our heads.

Afterwards, I myself
Hurried off to the airport
And into the sky.

*

Poetic Postscript: On *From the Air*

Poetic Postscript: On *From the Air*

We met as writers writing thinking about writing
worried about writing writing writing
In Iowa Writers' Workshop 1968 young men writing
Jews writing for Jews
Will write they will read and ponder text
Moved by wind or history or God's breath blown
backwards time or moving bodies the barely heard
hissing
Of the writing hand pagemind writing words worries
the hissing comes in swerving reflex, twitch of
words' echoes
For illumination of illusion that one's here that
something's to be done
What's to be done overtakes the Jew as person
What's to be done the question can't arise one's
moved
One can't know nor know one can't know that's so
In what it means washing over
so hissing worrying about words is worry hiss in soul
that's the same, God that's soul's hiss
is words swelling in snake's conspiratorial whispering
word, then obsession, desire, yes a body flesh an eye
a world to grope to grasp it's not there!
In such blindness approached what later we could not
but call religion in us
Not as religious people with settled faith but faith
unsettled blown back to
Approach religion as having fallen backward into it
worried about writing approach religion unsettled
Hissing as snake hiss am I I, what am I, what is
saying to say?

Found and lost young men seized by brutal life force
in them, pressed, pressure, blown back into God
Without what or why or where but moved by that
If not words can there be Jew, can there be God, religion?
No.
No, yes, first words.
A story going on
Makes time, lifetime like they say
Over face of deep, a word. There is light.
Arrangements of quiet words
Talking into the God

—

God in the beginning beyond beginning makes a beginning worries about words stamping image word onto world's indefinite vagueness that isn't yet or not or was/is/will be
With words words' utterance with Let there be with There is
The word's light the light's word there's "the" "it" there's "is" later "if"
The nothing hardened by words' hands reach out clutch grasp the nothing there
And there's worrying there then
Later persons to worry the worry…. Their story

—

In such wise were we swept by words but my words your words anyone's blathering on and on
My need my thought my hope my fear my awe/anguish

A trivial sea's multitudinous waves a wash a torrent
of words important important but my word your word
you think's yours anyone's word, no matter sea
sweeps it up it does not matter there's no matter
Matter's a word, words fly beyond words
Letters off pages into sky beyond sky into nothing
That's blankest of all words

—

His washed out to sea not once but twice three
times…. four
His life out of control
In control of others from the air
Leaving small words behind engraved on tablets
Hidden in basements. Drawers. Scrawled. On paper.
Not lost. Here.

—

God, actual God, appears in happenstance
Bright swagger of occurrence if you are helpless
To make your life, see it's made
You don't know what to do how could you know
what to do
Rules of grammar to be broken to gild the jar to
shatter
Out of control's religion what we call that to tame
that
See it's beyond knowing what to do, sink, fly
Sinking flying as one
Staggers blown backward falling into it, God's
restless sea — a word—

Washed out in it
Puts words in mouth so one's compelled, one's commanded
Shows images flicker screen of perception sounds as
Birds, messengers as angels all commanded
As written as parsed for their silences
Standing silent calm on tiptoe twirling
As lunatics twirl insisting

—

From bima a frame soaks through words
Even when as personal stories as there's humanness humor
It's God hidden as behind's the ark contains rolling scroll from whose flying washing words testifying
Words glow, permeating invisible sanctuary
In poems written in airports airplanes on highways cars
In conveyances moving always through space from air there
There's no time no frame the history's gone the collective dissolves into it
God's then in happenstance falling through thoughts as person in perception, sound
Worrying tinkering in words you express what what? Some human feeling? ?? It's the illusion of one
Matching the illusion of another as reading poems as persons
Worrying about words assuming words say what they mean refer to what's perceived
What one thinks feels what a person is one can imagine a person as one is

Yet God's absence soaks through
Memory soaks in it as blood
Always blood of the lost and gone the bludgeoned
burned the persecuted and the persecutor

—

They say Jews have long memory insist on that
That Jew is memory branded memory within which
Fervent wish to forget…
But no memory's not now
No now's not memorable, not happenstance
A Jew is a mystery to Jew to memory of Jew to
uttered words echoed hisssing
A Jew is for worrying about words words dazzled by
them broken open in them
They make them quiet they thunder in them they do
not know a word
For a word the word always moving one cannot hold
it still
This English not their language false language what's
their language it's erased
Resurrected not as Christ but as words but not the
same nothing is ever the same
Yet persons worrying about words remain in their
words erased
Preserved as if mirrors. Scrawled. On paper. Hidden.
Reflected. Here.
Then walked all the way out to sea's margins up and
down looks long long
Out at horizon of which end's, if end, indistinct

And if sky, from air's, none, the looking's look long
and long in the words erased

>Zuketsu Norman Fischer
>November 2021
>San Francisco, California

Hesped (Eulogy): in memory of Rabbi Alan Lew (*z″l*)

Hesped (Eulogy): in memory of Rabbi Alan Lew, *o.b.m.*

Pitchu Li Shaarei Tzedek Avo Vam Odeh Yah
Open for me the gates of rightness I will come to them I will praise God.

Zeh ha Shaar L'Adonai Tzadikkim Yavo u'Vo
This is the gate of Adonai, the righteous will go in.

(Psalm 118: 19-20)

It is difficult not to hear these words sung in Rabbi Lew's melodic voice. For many of us, we heard him sing them at so many Hallels at *Congregation Beth Sholom* or after a meditation session at *Makor Or*.

His daughters Hannah and Malka wanted this song to be sung at their father's funeral because it has been playing so persistently through their, and I imagine, many of our minds, in these days of our loss and grief.

I guess you could visualize these gates of righteousness in Psalm 118 as Heavenly doors waiting to accept our teacher, our friend, our rabbi:

> Open the Gates! Look who is here!
> Open them wide. Let the righteous enter.

As I hear this verse, I see an image of Rabbi Lew as he lived here, present and vital, among us, and I don't think of heavenly gates opening. I'd translate it: *Pitchu Li!* Open me! Open my heart.

When my heart is open, I will praise You. I will pass through every gate you show me. Keep allowing me to open my heart, wider and deeper, and I will keep going through this gate and the next and the next. As deep as I can know myself, so will I continue to find new ways to praise Your name. *Pitchu li!* Open my heart.

Rabbi Lew's life was lived with a generous, compassionate, open heart: rabbi, hospice chaplain, activist against the death penalty, author, pioneer of Jewish meditation, advocate for the homeless. Incomparable giver of sermons that made you think until you realized how deeply you felt his words. Words that stayed with you. As Malka said, "He felt everything. He felt everyone's pain. There were no boundaries to his heart. He kept his heart open."

Alan Jeffrey Lew was born on Staten Island on November 10, 1943, to Charlotte and Isaiah, "Icy," Lew. Icy was a successful dentist who invented dental implants and traveled the world lecturing about them. After doting on their first child, Alan, for three years, daughter Carol was born. Carol remembers Alan as a protective older brother who, despite loving her and teaching her to throw a baseball correctly, would make her walk 10 feet behind him on the way to the bus stop. She says, "He was always such a mixture." In high school, he was a football team captain, and, at the same time, a 17-year old sitting in his room writing poetry. Even then, she says, "He just wasn't like everyone else."

His brother Jason remembers Alan, seven years his senior, as funny, smart, and so handsome. They shared a bunk bed for many years and would grow up to share an interest in spirituality--practicing yoga and meditation. They also shared a love of music. Alan wrote beautiful songs and played the guitar very well, and Alan and Jason would sing harmonies together.

Winning a football scholarship to Penn, Alan didn't play ball but majored in English. It was there he met Betty, his first wife. After college, his father wanted Alan to go to medical school, but he fainted at the sight of blood. So, it was law school. After a year of study, Alan and Betty welcomed Steven to the world. Carol remembers that Alan doted on Steven, was infatuated with him.

Leaving law school before he finished, he worked as a newspaper reporter for the Yonkers Herald Statesman, tooling around on a red Vespa. But he longed to write stories, and went to the Iowa Writers' Workshop. There, in 1968, he met a fellow writing student, Norman Fischer. Norman said they were both wearing uniforms at the time: Norman's consisted of jeans, boots, a denim collarless shirt, and really long, wild hippie hair. Alan wore neatly pressed pants, a powder blue button down, belt, and neat shoes. Despite their different looks, they spent a lot of time together. Norman was jealous of Alan — he says, "I thought he was a better writer than I was. He had a wonderful careful touch with language and stories."

Norman tells a story about the depth of effect their friendship had on him: "When we were first friends in Iowa, I had never had a conversation ever with any of my male friends about our relationships together. At one point early in our friendship, it looked to Alan like I had taken up with other friends, neglecting him. He was very upset. I was astonished.

He had so much feeling. He expressed to me how much our friendship meant to him and how upset he was. I was so moved. No one else had ever done that in any human relationship I had before. It was a tremendous awakening for me. That he could care so much. And be hurt and speak it. It deepened our friendship. There was a different intensity and intentionality."

Intensity and intentionality.

Decades later, Norman and Alan would co-found *Makor Or*, a path-breaking Jewish Meditation center. Norman describes their partnership as harmonious, seamless, "it felt to both of us a real blessing."

After Iowa, Alan moved to Gualala, in Northern California. Writing, driving a bus, raising his son, he continued to deepen his meditation practice. His marriage to Betty ended.

It was during a Zen retreat at Tassajara, planning to deepen his commitment to Zen Buddhism, that Alan realized his was a Jewish soul. His ten years of disciplined Zen meditation was still a part of him, but he was about to find a new gate to enter and a partner to share the journey.

Sherril and Alan first saw each other during a reading that Sherril was giving at a club called the Grand Piano. She observed, from the stage, an extremely handsome man in a 3 piece suit (his Grayline bus driver uniform) with a face that was shining. He, meanwhile, was wondering what it might be like to be married to her. (He admitted later, that given the content of what she was reading, he was a little worried about her family).

They met, after several near misses, at a wedding. It was love at first sight. Sherril says, "I knew my *bashert,* even though I didn't know that word." They had a long conversation about their bubbies. Alan told Sherril, "I can get any bus driving job I want," and she understood it as code for telling her, "I will always protect you. I will always take care of you." They were engaged thirteen days later.

And theirs was a love story that lasted. Sherril calls Alan a complete husband, lover, companion, best friend. She says, "We were always happy to be together. He was extremely devoted. There were times life was not easy, but we were always incredibly in love. I felt loved always. He was the best possible husband. And everything I wrote was a love story to him." They celebrated their twenty-ninth wedding anniversary just recently over Hanukkah.

Their decision to have a rabbi officiate at their wedding, along with son Steven's desire to have a bar mitzvah, led them to Beth Ami, a Conservative synagogue in Santa Rosa, where they began to attend Torah study regularly. Almost immediately, Alan was trying to learn haftarah trop alongside his son and was giving weekly *divrei torah* on Shabbat. When the rabbi of the congregation left town, the congregants asked Alan to be their spiritual leader. He stayed on, but felt uncomfortable with his lack of Jewish knowledge. Alan went to the Jewish Theological Seminary in New York to interview for rabbinical school. The Dean encouraged him, but said, "I'm going to require you to join our Hebrew classes in Israel which begin in two weeks." At thirty-eight, with a son of bar mitzvah age, toddler Hannah, and weeks-old Malka, Alan called Sherril and said, "Hold on to your hat."

Without any significant Jewish educational background, Alan had to work diligently to keep up in rabbinical school. He worked so diligently he became a top student, a co-valedictorian. His parents, Charlotte and Icy, were tremendously proud of his decision to become a rabbi.

Alan worked and studied through six years of school, commuting to *Congregation Etz Chaim* in Monroe, New York, and working as the first chaplain of the *Jacob Perlow Hospice of Beth Israel Medical Center* in New York. His experience working in hospice profoundly affected him. He would later be a founding faculty member of the Metta Institute, providing education on spirituality in dying to caregivers. As a congregational rabbi, he saw hundreds of families through times of grief and provided spiritual care to the sick and wounded. Sherril recalls that "he felt it was a privilege to be called out of bed in the middle of the night to go sit with someone." And he would wake early, leaving the house to meet someone at 5 AM to pray with them before a surgery. He did this all the time.

Alan loved his children deeply. Malka calls him, "The best father I could ask for. He was made of pure love. He would always hug and kiss and tell us he loved us." Hannah remembers playing basketball with him and rooting alongside him for the Mets (though, of course, he would eventually switch to the Giants). After all, he had started out as a Dodgers fan. Lately, it was all about the Golden State Warriors (yes, I do know it is a different sport).

Hannah remembers her Dad sleeping with them in bed or on the floor next to them all night if she or Malka were scared. They loved swimming in the ocean with him when they visited their uncle Jason on Martha's Vineyard. He would go into the freezing water when no other adult would dare, and let them and all the cousins swim on his back. More recently, Hannah spent time with her father helping him to organize his papers and going to art galleries and museums. Steve remembers his dad teaching him to play guitar, and how his father took Steven's somewhat rebellious request to explore Judaism, and have a Bar Mitzvah, and completely overtook what had been "my thing."

He was a hard worker and gave of himself so much. To everyone. And then he would come home and crash. He would run out of energy—drained—and need to zone out. Sherril laughs that they didn't often have Shabbat guests because "when Alan would return from shul he would fall asleep with his head in the soup."

"Your Dad changed my life," is something Malka has heard many times. He sent so many otherwise normal people to become rabbis. He influenced so many lives. Recently, her Dad encouraged her to meditate, so that she could find her own truth and center. He loved it when she joined him for morning meditation, and on the walk back, he would say things like, "Did you see how beautiful the sky is right now? Did you see that tree?"

With his beloved granddaughters, Sema and Ayla, Alan was a "beyond indulgent" Zayde. Steve recalls telling Alan that Sema reads fairy books and might like one for Hanukkah. He came home with 30 books.

After graduation from rabbinical school, the Lew family moved to Monroe, New York, where his part-time student pulpit offered him a full-time job. After two years of full-time duties, the congregation had doubled in size. But Alan had another gate to enter, and, shortly after telling his congregation that he would be leaving, he discovered that *Beth Sholom*, a big conservative synagogue in San Francisco, was looking for a rabbi. From 1991-2005, Rabbi Lew was the spiritual leader, the heart, of *Congregation Beth Sholom*. For fourteen years, he inspired, educated, provoked, and pushed us all.

He was inventive, inspiring, intellectual. Rabbi Lew made us laugh and think and cry. He didn't mind repeating the same jokes, and we didn't mind laughing each time. I can't read *Parshat Beshallach* without thinking of Rabbi Lew's great discovery. He uncovered the true identity of the manna, that famously white, malleable, nutritious food which nourished the Children of Israel in the wilderness. Hiding in the Hebrew verb for baking, this miraculous food was "tofu." He would remind us that we in California could be proud of our vegetarian cuisine's Biblical heritage.

I can admit now that sometimes Rabbi Lew was so funny and clever in off-hand comments while we sat next to each other on the *bimah* at services, we, quite rightly, got shushed by the Board President.

But those sermons. How many of us looked forward to hearing what he was going to say each Shabbat? Each High Holiday season? How many people left his teaching with a renewed respect not just for this one rabbi but for a sophisticated and deeply relevant Jewish tradition? How many people left his teaching angry! He didn't hold back, and he wasn't afraid to confront uncomfortable truths. As he would say, "If you haven't changed your mind at least once, you haven't attempted to grasp the complexity of the situation."

Rabbi Lew loved Torah. He loved learning and he loved teaching. He was a brilliant interpreter of texts, with an un-erring ability to find the emotional content, the heart, behind the letters of the text. He used his immense intellect not to impress you but to impress on you the possibilities of a life deeply and attentively lived.

In his last sermon at *Beth Sholom* before becoming Rabbi Emeritus, he talked about these possibilities of authentic living in relation to his commitment to LGBT advocacy. "This is one of the reasons the cause of gay and lesbian Jews became so important to me during my tenure here... *Al regal echat*, on one foot, Judaism is precisely about becoming who we are, about realizing our deepest potential, about manifesting the divine spark of self that God has implanted within us....I don't think the rest of us have a sufficient appreciation for how much courage it takes to be who you really are when the world by and large doesn't want you to be. And I don't think the rest of us have sufficient appreciation for the degree to which gays and lesbians have been fighting our most important battles for us, because each of us struggles to express who we are, each of us knows the temptation of betraying our deepest self for the sake of the approval and admiration of others, and far too many of us squander the divine gift that is given to us *bizroah netunah*—on God's outstretched arm — every moment of our life."

His work with *Religious Witness with the Homeless*, sleeping in the park, being arrested protesting the demolition of a housing project was a part of his recognizing that everyone has this divine gift. As was his advocacy opposing the death penalty, a towering presence at night through to the early hours of the morning, calling out names of those executed and the names of those the executed killed at each execution at San Quentin since his Bay area return.

He saw and wanted to protect and encourage the divine gift given to each of us *bi'zroah netunah*—on God's outstretched arm—every moment of our life. He did not betray his gift. His divine gift was not squandered. It was shared. Generously. With an open heart.

For decades, pursuing and excelling in the rabbinate, pioneering Jewish meditation, growing a family, tirelessly advocating for those without a voice, moderating Mosaic, a television program, presiding over the Northern California Board of Rabbis, meeting other religious leaders who had experience with more than one faith in conferences in Italy and Spain, scholar-in-residence talks, all these activities kept him rather busy.

Still, he was always there for others. He was such a support to me in my work and my life. Always a mentor, always a cheerleader. Rabbi Tracy Nathan, who flew in from Boston for 24 hours in order to be here, told me that after her first Rosh Hashanah sermon at *Beth Sholom*, she returned to her seat on the bimah, and Rabbi Lew leaned over to say, "You hit it out of the ballpark, kiddo." We marveled together at the strength of his charm: neither of us was ever bothered by being called kiddo. We loved it.

The book he had started to write about his family's stories decades before, the book he felt he needed to write, sat without attention. He wrote three other books first, co-authoring *One God Clapping* with Sherril. Just last year, Rabbi Lew finished *The Life That Ran Through Me*.[34] Decades of work. He told me he felt a tremendous sense of peace after finishing it.

His long-time friend, Norman, said of Alan: "His life was complete. He did his work." Rabbi Lew, my teacher, my mentor, and my friend, sat me down in his office when I first came to *Beth Sholom* to orient me to how he performed life cycle rituals. I titled this folder, unbeknownst to him, "How to be Rabbi Lew." Reviewing my file last night, I saw that he told me the point of a eulogy is "If you had to stand on one foot: What was this life about? Why was this person sent to this planet?" (Can't you hear him saying that?)

You who have come here today, along with thousands who have been touched through his teaching, his books, or personal interactions in hospitals, *huppahs*, homes—each of you know what he brought to you. How he brought you closer to Torah,

---

[34] *The Life That Ran Through Me* was completed by Lew in 2008 and remains to be published.

closer to the truth of a moment, closer to seeking or knowing your own divine gift, or just, in an important time, with a word or a smile or a hug, how he brought you close.

Perhaps his gift was to remind us, through his words and his actions, that we have so many avenues, so many gateways available to us to explore and engage our own God-given gifts. Torah study, meditation, activism, writing, prayer, healing and investing in relationships with friends and family, he showed us, are gates to opening the heart. And an open heart is the key to entering ever more profound and powerful gateways.

After hearing of his death on Monday, I picked up *One God Clapping*. I started reading some of his old sermons. I think I started this reading because I wanted to feel connected to him, to hear his voice. I found, as I kept reading, that he had pulled me in. What came from his heart was still entering mine, leading me towards a search for the answers to the questions he raised. I read in *One God Clapping*:

> "My name, Lew, was actually pronounced "Lev," in Poland where my Zayde Isaac was born. The Polish letter that sounds like a V looks like an English W, however, and when Isaac came through Ellis Island, they changed his name to "Lew." In Hebrew, Lev means 'heart'."

Pithu li, Open me, Open my heart to the gates of rightness, and I will praise You. This is the gate for the righteous, I will go inside.

Malka believes that her father's heart was open so wide to the world, that, finally, it burst. He was so generous with his love and his time. So many of us, having a taste of it, wanted more and more.

You opened your heart to us, Rabbi Lew, and as the Talmud says, "What comes from the heart enters the heart." We, each of us, carry words and images of you that will continue to inspire and console us, even after your death, even in our grief.

This is real. And we are totally unprepared. I wish you could have stayed a while longer. I wasn't ready to say goodbye. But, though your life wasn't long enough, you hit it out of the ballpark. Shalom, rabi u'mori. Goodbye to my teacher, my rabbi, my friend.

Yehi zichro baruch.
May his memory be for a blessing.

Rabbi Dorothy Richman
December 2021
Berkeley, California

ABOUT THE AUTHOR:

Alan Jeffry Lew was born in Brooklyn in 1943. When he was seven, he moved with his family to Usonia, an intentional community founded by Frank Lloyd Wright in Westchester County, New York. He went to the University of Pennsylvania, The Iowa Writers' Workshop, and The Jewish Theological Seminary. but for ten years before he went to the seminary he practiced Buddhism in Berkeley, California. His first pulpit was Eitz Chaim in Monroe, New York; his next and last, Congregation Beth Sholom in San Francisco. He was known for the brilliance of his sermons and his tender and conscientious pastoral care. He was known for his social action. With Norman Fischer he founded Makor Or, the first Jewish mediation center attached to a synagogue, on the idea that simple mindfulness meditation could prepare one for prayer. He died suddenly at the age of sixty-five, in 2009, after just completing what he considered to be his life's work, a family saga he called *The Life That Ran Through Me*. He is also author of: *This Is Real and You Are Completely Unprepared: The Days of Awe As a Journey of Transformation.* (2018); *One God Clapping: The Spiritual Path of a Zen Rabbi.* (2014); *Be Still and Get Going: A Jewish Meditation Practice for Real Life* (2005). He is survived by his widow, the writer, Sherril Jaffe, his children, Stephen, Hannah, and Malka, and his grandchildren, Sema, Ayla, and Emmett.

PANUI TITLES
www.panui.org

Elliot R. Wolfson, *Unveiling the Veil of Unveiling: Philosophical Aphorisms & Poems on Time, Language, Being, & Truth* (2022).

Eitan Fishbane, *Embers of Pilgrimage* (2021).

Aubrey L. Glazer, *God Knows, Everything Is Broken: the Great (Gnostic) Americana Songbook of Bob Dylan* (2019).

Aubrey L. Glazer & Nehemia Polen, editors, *From Tiberias, with Love: A Collection of Tiberian Hasidism*: **Volume 2: R. Abraham ha-Kohen of Kalisk** (2020).

Aubrey L. Glazer & Nehemia Polen, editors, *From Tiberias, with Love: A Collection of Tiberian Hasidism*: **Volume 1: R. Menachem Mendel of Vitebsk** (2019).

Made in the USA
Middletown, DE
15 March 2022